AF176190

Nadja Kalinowski

BABY & DOG

HOW DO I BEST PREPARE MY DOG FOR THE BABY?

A GUIDE FOR A RELAXED LIFE TOGETHER

Impressum

Bibliografische Information der Deutschen Nationalbibliothek:
Die Deutsche Nationalbibliothek verzeichnet diese Publikation
in der Deutschen Nationalbibliografie; detaillierte
bibliografische Daten sind im Internet über http://dnb.dnb.de
abrufbar.

© 2022 Nadja Kalinowski

Herstellung und Verlag: BoD – Books on Demand,
Norderstedt

ISBN: 9783756210664

Table of Contents

I

About me

Welcome! I'm so glad you found this book. My name is Nadja Kalinowski (www.trustandlead.de) and I would like to introduce myself:

My path as a professional dog psychologist began in 2013. At that time my male dog Milo was 3 years old and my female dog Lefi was 1 years old. Both dogs are completely different and have challenged me in different areas.

Milo tends to be a loner and very self-confident in many situations. If he is barked at by other dogs on the leash, it does not interest him at all. As a terrier, he wants to be challenged and needs clear rules and structure.

His individual distance, which is the personal distance that he needs to have from strange dogs in order to feel comfortable, is very high. If this is not respected, it may be that he demands distance from the other dog which he will communicate. However, this also causes stress for him.

Over time I learned to understand Milo and his behavior. I can now relieve him of the stress that it is causing him and control the situations for him. In addition, it is nice to see how his trust in me has grown more and more as a result.

Lefi was a hyperactive bundle of energy in her early years. She could not stay alone or walk relaxed on a leash. Her initial panic and fear of dogs didn't make going for walks any easier.

At that time we lived in the middle of Hamburg, Germany with constantly new attractions in front of the door. That was an additional challenge for the training. With a lot of patience and commitment, we were able to successfully work on her issues.

Despite her issues, Lefi's lovely and sweet nature has already helped many children to overcome their fear of dogs. She teaches how to deal with dogs and imparts knowledge in a playful way in kindergarten classrooms and schools.

Through my own experiences with my dogs, I know how my clients feel and how hard the road can be at times.

My dogs have taught me so much. I am grateful for the valuable lessons, especially on the topics of trust and leadership. My learning never stops. I can learn something new from every dog I get to work with.

I now pass on my accumulated knowledge in the field of dog psychology to my customers in the form of online-, home sessions or workshops.

More info: www.trustandlead.de

Training example (true story)

The phone rang, I got a frantic call and headed straight for an emergency training. At the front door I was greeted by a barking Jack Russell Terrier. The woman had a crying newborn in her arms and it was clear to see that the couple were at the end of their wits.

We began with the session and I first started by observing. The dog didn't rest during my stay, he was extremely tense the entire time. The child's screams obviously put him in a hunting mode again and again. He could only be kept away from the baby with a leash.

The parents told me that the day before the baby and dog first met, the dog stood over the baby and stared at her. The situation was very serious and unfortunately my prognosis was not good.

We immediately started setting up rules and developing a concrete training plan. Giving up was not (yet) an option for the couple. Baby and dog weren't allowed to get together for the foreseeable future. I left the couple with a bad feeling.

After a week I came back and was pleasantly surprised. The father kept to all agreements and trained diligently. He slept with the dog in the living room and the woman slept in the bedroom with the baby.

The dog was no longer recognizable. Under my supervision, we reunited baby and dog, with the dog being relaxed this time. There were clear rules that gave the dog the necessary rest.

The dog politely approached the baby this time and picked up the scent. He no longer fell into his hunting behavior when the baby was screaming and was now controllable in all situations. A huge weight fell of my shoulders. I would not have thought such an extreme change in behavior was possible in such a short time, but the owners surpassed themselves.

My work was done and I wished the little family well. They were relieved and overjoyed. Months later, positive news reached me with photos of the relaxed baby & dog.

However, the situation could have turned out very differently.

Hallo Nadja, wir wollten uns nochmal bei dir Bedanken da du uns Anfang des Jahres ja so toll geholfen hast und dir einen Weihnachtsvideogruß senden. 🎅🎄 Pepe und die Keine verstehen sich wirklich super. Der Hund ist ganz lieb und vorsichtig und alles ist gut.Sie spielen täglich, indem sie ihm Dinge bringt🐶❤️LG
🐶Pepe

10:2

„Hello Nadja, we wanted to thank you because you helped us so much at the beginning of the year and sent you Christmas greetings. Pepe and the little one get along really well. The dog is very sweet and careful and everything is fine. They play daily by her bringing him things. Warm greetings"

The sooner you start training your dog and preparing him for the changes, the easier it will be for you to adjust once the baby arrives.

This saves you and your dog a lot of stress. Unfortunately, there is no guarantee that it will actually work properly, but this way you don't have to blame yourself later for not having done enough.

If there is a serious danger, persistent stress or excessive demands due to the additional workload, the "worst case" must be considered.

Since I get such requests, including short-term emergency training, more often now, I decided to create a baby & dog program and write it down here.

This program contains all the necessary preparations before the baby arrives, with exercises for the dog and instructions for the first time together.

Of course, you should always look at your dog individually, but with this book you get an overview and instructions on many different topics.

My goal for you: A stress-free and happy life together.

Introduction

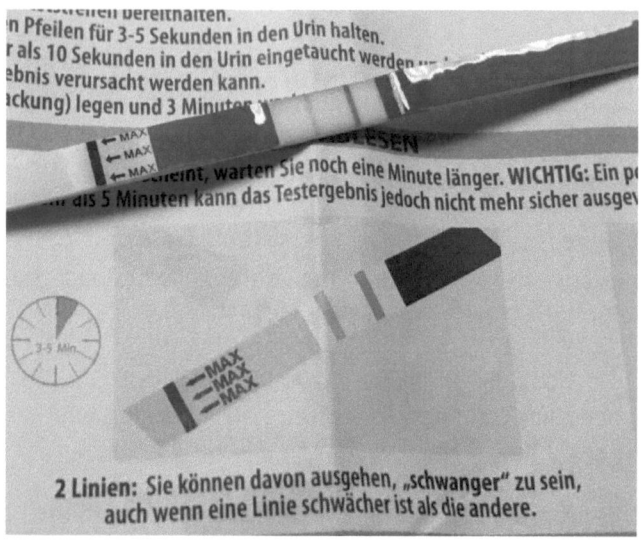

...~~~~~ bereithalten.
'n Pfeilen für 3-5 Sekunden in den Urin halten.
r als 10 Sekunden in den Urin eingetaucht werden ...
ebnis verursacht werden kann.
ackung) legen und 3 Minut...

...~~int, warten Sie noch eine Minute länger. WICHTIG: Ein p...
... als 5 Minuten kann das Testergebnis jedoch nicht mehr sicher ausge...

3-5 Min.

2 Linien: Sie können davon ausgehen, „schwanger" zu sein, auch wenn eine Linie schwächer ist als die andere.

Did you get the happy news that you are expecting a baby? Congratulations, this is the start of an exciting time.

So far your dog has gotten your undivided attention and you may have some thoughts such as:

- how it will work out with the baby?

- feel a little unsure what to look out for or?

- just want to prepare as best you can?

These are all very normal and good thoughts to have because there are already some exercises that you should do with your dog during pregnancy!

Use this time to prepare your dog for the changes. This saves you and your dog a lot of stress when the baby is here. By doing these exercises, it gives you the advantage that your dog doesn't link the changes to the baby because they have already started before that.

Your life will change completely and so will your dog's life. Nowadays it is often the case that the dog has taken a very close place at our side. The dog is an important member of the family and for some people also a "child". As long as the dog doesn't have to share the space and attention, this can be fine. But now that another family member is moving in, we want this to be as stress free as possible for EVERYONE.

Have you already had the baby and are you noticing changes in your dog?

Of course, you can still do all the exercises described here with your dog. If your child is in danger, please get support from an experienced trainer.

In this book we start with the basics and then work our way to the specific topics related to babies and dogs.

self assessment

In order for you to know how your current status with your dog is, you should make an honest self-assessment. Take your time to answer the questions. Watch yourself and your feelings.

Do some questions make you feel uncomfortable?

With your answers, you can then proceed more specifically in the training and know which topics you have to pay particular attention to.

Important questions for you in advance:

How would you rate the character of your dog?

Is he confident and relaxed? Sensitive to anxious or rather bold and demanding?

....
....
....
....
....
....
....

How does your dog react to

loud noises?

....
....
....
....
....
....
....

sudden movements?

....
....
....
....
....
....
....

or touches?

....
....
....
....
....
....
....

Does your dog pay close attention to your mood?

....
....
....
....
....
....
....
....

What is the level of training?

....
....
....
....
....
....
....

Are you meeting your dog's needs?

....
....
....
....
....
....
....
....

How much physical exercise does your dog need?

....
....
....
....
....
....
....

How much mental exercise does your dog need?

....
....
....
....
....
....
....

Do you already have problems with your dog (jumping, barking, stealing food or objects, being stressed alone, territorial behavior...)?

....
....
....
....
....
....
....

Have you already worked on the topics?

How do you assess the change and the current status?

....
....
....
....
....
....
....
....

Does your dog know babies and/or children?

How is he doing there?

....
....
....
....
....
....
....
....
....
....
....
....
....
....

How do you feel about the thought of baby & dog? Are you more insecure, nervous, anxious or relaxed?

....
....
....
....
....
....
....

Does your dog show threatening behavior towards other people or you (growling, holding still)?

....
....
....
....
....
....
....

Has your dog already snapped or bitten? What were the situations?

....
....
....
....
....
....
....

Would things be different today?

....
....
....
....
....
....
....

Is your dog controlling or defending you?

E.g. constantly following you, stepping in when someone hugs you?

....
....
....
....
....
....
....

Is your dog possessive, e.g. with food or toys?

....
....
....
....
....
....
....

How does your dog react to changes (e.g. in the daily routine)?

....
....
....
....
....
....
....

How does your dog behave at family gatherings or meetings with friends?

....
....
....
....
....
....
....

What role has your dog played in your life so far?

....
....
....
....
....
....
....
....

Space for additional notes:

....
....
....
....
....
....
....
....
....
....
....
....
....
....
....
....
....
....
....
....
....
....
....
....
....
....
....

Multi- dog household

If you have more than one dog at home, then please answer these questions honestly:

How do your dogs get along with each other?

....
....
....
....
....
....
....

Are there fights between the dogs? If so, what are the triggers (food, toys, you)?

....
....
....
....
....
....
....

Did someone get hurt? Injuries?

....
....
....
....

....
....
....

Are the dogs vying for your attention?

....
....
....
....
....
....
....

Do the dogs know that you lead the pack?

....
....
....
....
....
....
....

If the dogs fight or fight over you, this can mean not only stress but also danger for your baby. From the dogs' point of view, a new competitor could be added.

Note: You do not belong to anyone but yourself!

You're very good at taking care of yourself. You provide the pack with food, shelter, exercise, affection, and (hopefully) meet the needs of your dogs. As the leader of your pack, you don't tolerate friction around you.

Work on your leadership skills and consistently implement what you have learned here. It is very important that you pay attention to your energy. A pack leader is calm but assertive. There is no such thing as an insecure, nervous, angry, frustrated, anxious, excited pack leader among dogs.

These emotions radiate weakness, but your dog needs your inner strength.

Consider precautions

As already mentioned, it is highly recommended to start making changes before the baby is born.

In this way, your dog does not associate them with the new family member, but it is already the normal state when the baby arrives.

Since we don't know how your dog will be like with the baby and how stressful it will be, it's important to consider precautions.

Remember that your dog also reacts to your mood. Depending on the nature of the dog, it can react very sensitively to stress, a baby cries or your insecurity.

We want EVERYONE to feel comfortable in the future. The precautionary measures are not only for you and the baby, but also for your dog/dogs.

Three important recommendations that you can implement NOW!

Recommendation number 1: Fixed resting place

When things get stressful and hectic, it's important that your dog has a quiet and safe zone. Especially when your dog starts to take on tasks that are not intended for him, e.g.:

- take care of the baby

- exaggerated territorial behavior among visitors

- control of people (e.g. by constantly chasing)

- begging at the table

It will be a huge help for you if you can send your dog to his place in all kinds of situations and he relaxes there.

In order to make it as easy as possible for the dog, the optimal sleeping and resting place is an important point.

It should be a quiet place to retreat and relax. It is best not to be right next to the TV/radio speakers or the children's play area.

Often a reason why the dog cannot relax is because the sleeping place is a control position (e.g. a place directly overlooking the entrance area).

Air traffic controllers can't just go to sleep at an airport in the tower, can they?

For example, if your dog is laying in the middle of the hallway, with all the doors and a view of you constantly in sight, it cannot get the rest and sleep it urgently needs.

Caution: If disregarded, it can even lead to danger with some dogs. When your dog is at his sleeping place, strangers or visitors do not have to disturb him there.

Even if your dog finds being disturbed by familiar people uncomfortable, that is okay and MUST be respected. Your dog should learn that his place is his quiet and safe zone, where he can rest.

Give your dog great treats and chews at his resting place. On the one hand, chewing calms the dog, on the other hand, it connects the place with something great.

Does your dog keep getting up?

Use your body language. Make yourself tall and send your dog back. Warn him with a sound when he wants to get up. After a disregarded warning, the consequence follows, e.g. by bringing the dog back to its place with the leash.

Is your dog too fast for you?

Then use a house leash to help you. It is like an extended arm that allows you to easily bring your dog back to his resting place.

A lot of repetition and patience is very important here! Don't get emotional!

Is your dog used to making his own decisions? Then it may very well be that you will first discuss it with him. Hang in there, he's testing you. He won't just leave the lead to you, you have to prove to him that you can do it.

Important: If you have actively sent your dog to its resting place, it must remain there until you release it.

Remember: You make the decision, not your dog.

If possible, pay no attention to your dog (look at, speak to, touch) when he is at his resting place. Otherwise, you are looking for communication with your dog and he will probably get up or not manage to relax.

We don't ask much of your dog just that he relaxes in his resting place where he is safe and comfortable. Do not release your dog until he is relaxed.

When is your dog relaxed?

When he is (almost) asleep or the body is on its side and the head is down. By dissolving into relaxation, your dog will learn that this behavior is exactly what is desired.

Release your dog calmly so that you don't ruin the relaxation you've worked out with excitement. You can make a welcoming hand gesture or sit down and gently pet him as a reward.

Releasing with a command that creates excitement usually leads to expectations in your dog. This expectation does not allow him to associate the place of rest with relaxation, but with waiting.

Crate

Many dogs love to have a crate and many people feel guilty about putting the dog in a crate.

A crate is like a cave for the dog, it gives him security. If your dog poses a risk in some situations, please use the box to help.

Especially when your child starts to crawl and interact more with the dog, you protect not only your child but also your dog with the crate.

The crate also gives you a feeling of security, especially in circumstances that you cannot control. It can help you control situations when you have to go into another room or quickly to the door.

Crate training

Start feeding your dog in the crate so that he associates it positively. Then slowly start opening and closing the door. Do not close the door until your dog relaxes. Be next to the crate to begin with and only start moving away when your dog is calm. Leaving him in the crate in an excited state of mind will make him feel trapped. Take your time and be patient.

Remember: Our goal is a relaxed dog.

It is best to start crate training when your dog has been outside and has eaten, i.e. is tired. The fatigue will help you and him to associate the crate with relaxation more quickly. It is also helpful to let the dog sleep in its crate at night. Remember, the crate is a beautiful place for your dog, his own home.

Info: In multi-dog households, each dog should have its own resting place and/or crate.

Recommendation number 2: Bed/ sofa not freely accessible

First of all: I have no problem with the dog being on the sofa or bed. In fact, contact laying is important to the relationship between you and your dog. However, I think it is important that your dog is not uninvited on your bed/sofa.

This also has something to do with respect. In the best case, you also respect your dog's bed and do not disturb him there.

Another important point is that it can be dangerous if, for example, you are breastfeeding the baby and your dog just jumps on you. It would be much nicer if he was relaxed and then you invited him over to you for a cuddle, wouldn't it?

Are you wondering whether and how you should implement all of this?

Start today!

Whenever your dog jumps onto the sofa/bed uninvited, you bring him back down. Yes always. Your commitment and consistency are required. Some dogs can be very persistent, so be patient.

If your dog is very stubborn and quick, use a house-leash as an aid.

With the help of the house leash, you can easily get your dog off the sofa/bed again.

Remember to be calm and assertive. Don't let yourself be provoked; you don't need to get emotional about it.

The transition is usually harder for the owner than for the dog. If your dog makes extreme demands on the sofa/bed, I recommend that you ban the sofa and bed for at least 2 weeks.

Keep the big final goal in mind: A relaxed life with baby & dog.

The more your dog questions the new rule, the more you seem to have to earn respect as a pack leader.

Outlook for the future: It is very likely that you will soon have more children to visit you. Some children are insecure or even anxious around dogs. Even better if they can sit on your sofa without the dog harassing them. This will help them lose their fear of your dog.

Recommendation number 3: Child gate

Install child gates in the children's room, possibly in other rooms where your child is not constantly supervised.

Is there already a children's room?

This is your child's future kingdom. Here it should be able to move freely and spread out its toys. A place where your dog does not have to have access.

To make it easier for you, use a child gate. This is also often easier for the dog. So he can still see something and be there, despite the closed child gate. That would not be possible with the room door.

Maybe it makes sense that your dog also learns with other rooms that he shouldn't go in there?

For example, you could as well introduce this for the bathroom and/or the kitchen. You don't need a child gate, but it makes the practice process easier. In addition, it is also a good safety measure for baby & dog.

Since your baby will spend a lot of time with you in the first few years, you should consider whether you should additionally secure areas in the living room or bedroom. One possibility would be a grid, which you can flexibly rearrange for e.g. the changing area or the play blanket.

Those were the first three recommendations you can start practicing with your dog **NOW**.

Let's focus on the foundation. Be honest with yourself and see what you are already doing and what you still need to work on. This is how we prepare your dog optimally for the baby.

Exercise

How much mental and physical exercise your dog needs depends on:

- Age

- Energy level (calm, active or very active)

- Breed

- Health status

A senior will need less exercise than a youngster and a Weimaraner probably more than a pug. But no matter what breed, the important thing is the energy level. Is your dog quiet or very active? Depending on it, he requires more or less exercise.

Mental exercise

Challenging the dog mentally: This means challenging his brain and not just his body. Mental exercise includes, for example, teaching tricks or commands, but also impulse control exercises.

Impulse control is about self-control. This can be, for example, with exercises so that your dog will learn not to follow all distractions.

My favorite exercise for doing this is sending the dog to the resting place and then adding various distractions.

Distractions could be: placing or even moving toys or food on the floor, being in motion yourself (making strange movements, jumping, dancing), ...

Anything that might tempt your dog to get up and where he needs to control himself. This exercise is very exhausting for many dogs. Always finish the exercise calmly and reward your dog when he makes good decisions. Don't ask too much of your dog, one step at a time.

Teaching the dog commands or tricks

When training commands, tricks or things that are unnatural from the dog's point of view (e.g. brushing, cutting claws, checking teeth, putting on a dog jacket), I like to use classic dog training.

Otherwise, I orientate myself in my work to the aspects of dog psychology, the natural way. I observe how the dogs communicate and interact with each other. I then apply that to my work.

But since I haven't seen one dog teach another to put on a dog jacket, I choose the human way here.

The focus is on having fun!

What is important for dog training?

The right reward:

What does your dog like, what motivates your dog to do something with/for you?

For most dogs I know, the best reward is:

Food

Take small and preferably soft treats that your dog can chew quickly. If you have treats that are too big or hard, then your dog will be more concerned with chewing than learning the trick. If the treats smell nice, that's extra motivation. However, remember to adjust the amount of food according to the additional treats given.

Toy

Is your dog more likely to be motivated by toys? No problem.

For some dogs, praise by voice or stroking is enough. So first find out what motivates your dog.

Clicker

For harder tricks, I like to use a secondary amp, the clicker. It is important that you condition your dog for the clicker first. This means that the dog knows that after each click the reward follows.

Yes, even if you've made a mistake. With this tool you can very precisely confirm the desired behavior of your dog, e.g. the paw should be in a certain position during a trick.

Timing

You have about 1.5 seconds to reward your dog for the behavior. If you take longer, your dog can no longer associate this with the desired action and, in the worst case, you will reward other behavior.

The same applies to punishment, by the way. Many people scold their dog when they come home because, for example, they broke something while they were away. They then assume that the dog knows exactly what it has done. He often only reacts to the mood of the owner and therefore shows submissive behavior.

The dog no longer associates your behavior with its misconduct. This leads us directly to the next point:

Your mood

Only train your dog if you really feel like it. If you are annoyed, frustrated or even angry, your dog will notice it immediately and, in the worst case, link it to the training. Practicing commands or tricks should be fun and take place in a relaxed atmosphere.

Time

Take your time and don't do the exercises if you're in a hurry. Your dog needs as long as he needs. A lot of small repetitions are important and also stopping when the dog has mastered the exercise.

If your dog starts squeaking, scratching, biting, or showing other changes in behavior, this is usually a sign that he is overwhelmed. You probably practiced with him too long or were incomprehensible to him. By that I mean he doesn't know what you want from him.

Try to simplify your exercises and break it down into many small steps.

Practicing tricks or commands is very tiring mental work for your dog. Most dogs can only train a few minutes. If possible, end an exercise after a positive result or reduce the requirement so that you can end positively.

Do you remember when you wrote a test at school?

You were also tired afterwards, even though you didn't do any physical activity. This is how your dog feels when it comes to mental workload.

Please also remember that your command has to be repeated MANY times before your dog really understands it reliably.

Then name the command with one word. He should associate the word with the action you want.

The right place to practice

Please remember to practice in different places so that your dog can do the trick not only in the living room afterwards. Start in low-stimulus environments so your dog can focus.

As little distraction as possible is ideal. It is best to start at home and if the exercises there work reliably, you move the training outside.

Does your dog start barking, squeaking, scratching, jumping or overexcited when it is mentally busy?

These can be signs of being overwhelmed. As I said, end the unit on a positive note, because often less is more.

Questions to ask yourself if your dog shows excessive demands:

Have you clearly communicated to your dog what you want from him?

Was the session too long?

Were the distractions too big?

Was your dog already tired?

Were you calm and relaxed?

Impulse control

In addition to the commands & tricks, impulse control is very important.

This means that your dog can control himself and can handle frustration.

Especially when your baby starts to become more mobile, your dog must be able to accept not being involved. You will find more on this topic further on.

Physical exercise,

these include, for example, walking, jogging, cycling or dog sports.

Caution: Please do not turn your dog into a high-performance athlete!

A combination of mental and physical exercise with sufficient breaks is best. As a result, your dog is balanced and can rest at home.

Rest & Sleep

Sufficient rest and sleep are also very important for dogs and the topic is often underestimated. Too little sleep leads to hyperactivity, irritability, and makes your dog more susceptible to illness.

Especially with puppies and young dogs, it can be observed that they increasingly bite the owner`s hands or objects, destroy something, run around wildly, possibly injure themselves or other problems arise.

These are often signs that they are not getting enough sleep or that it's time for a break. Puppies and young dogs in particular need peace and quiet to be able to process everything they have experienced.

Please help your dog get the breaks he needs. I have often experienced that the owners misinterpret this behavior and then want to exercise the dog even more. The result is overwhelmed owners with totally overtired and overexcited dogs.

Are you unsure whether your dog has enough rest periods? I recommend a sleep diary to get a better overview.

Some dogs need to be taught to rest.

As with children, not every dog takes a nap voluntarily, even if it is good and necessary for him.

Adult dogs with sleep deprivation can also become more irritable and can lead to the dog possibly showing aggressive behavior.

In the case of rather insecure dogs, too little rest can be expressed through particularly anxious behavior.

We don't do well either if we don't sleep enough. Some people are then in a bad mood, lack concentration or develop health problems.

Make sure that your dog not only rests, but also sleeps during the day. Prepare your dog now that he can sleep in another room. When the baby is here, the nights will be restless, even for your dog. All the better if he can then withdraw and sleep stress-free in the next room.

By using a well-thought-out daily structure with enough rest and sleep phases, I have already been able to help many customers and their dogs change problematic behavior. Try it!

Rituals & Boundaries

Clear and understandable rules, rituals and boundaries make life easier for a dog as they provide security and orientation.

I still find that many owners find it difficult to set limits for the dog.

The idea that a dog should have freedom is a common argument. However, most dogs are overwhelmed with too much freedom and don't make good decisions themselves.

In addition, freedom is a privilege. Isn't it much nicer to experience something together with the dog than many meters apart?

I often experience this in a pack when I'm with the dogs in a large meadow. They could go far away, but instead they willingly stay close to me.

In nature, the pack stays together even without the other dogs having treats or a leash.

Rules & boundaries are very natural for dogs and also necessary. If you don't lead him, he has to take the lead, whether or not he can or wants to. Many dogs are overwhelmed with the leadership role and this creates problem behavior.

How is your dog supposed to know what's going on in the "human world", what's allowed and what's not?

Your child will also have to follow rules designed to keep them safe. For example: You stop when you see red, and you can walk when you see green. Your child will first have to learn these rules and you will practice it with them.

So why not set rules for the dog too and thus relieve him of responsibility?

I like to remind you that our goal is a relaxed dog.

Rules and boundaries are an important part of this. Your dog won't love you any less because of it.

On the contrary, he will start looking up to you and orienting himself towards you.

Having set rules = taking responsibility for the outcome of your dog's behavior.

Take the lead, your dog will thank you!

What does leadership mean?

Leadership is about trust and the ability to give and follow directions. It also has to do with being fair in the demands you make. The leader of the pack is calm but determined.

So you shouldn't get emotional when you ask something of your dog. Dogs are very smart and sense our mood. You can't fool your dog. He knows you very well.

You don't get the leadership position for free; you have to work for it and prove for the life of a dog that you can do it well. Every day, all day.

10 suggestions for your home

1. Daily routine

A regular daily routine is particularly important for insecure dogs. This means fixed activity and rest times that give the dog security. Especially when things get hectic with the child, it's good if your dog knows that it's time to rest.

2. Check doors and narrow areas (e.g. hallway)

Who goes through the door first? From today on, you do! This applies when leaving and also when coming back. Why? When you go out, you lead your dog and check the territory. When you come home, you enter your territory first - not the other way around.

Also make sure that your dog does not lay in narrow areas such as the hallway. This could lead to uncomfortable situations later with the child, as your dog may feel trapped in the narrow space. Show him that he has his peace in his dog bed or crate.

3. Clear the way

Is your dog is in the way and you walk around it? Please make sure that you don't avoid your dog but that he gives you the space.

If he blocks your way with his body, don't take a detour but let him go to the side. He should respect your space and instead of laying in the way, he should rest in his dog bed/ crate.

4. Structure on the walk

Whoever walks in the front, leads. Who makes the decisions when to sniff or pee? How fast/slow to go or where to run to? From today it's you!

5. Waiting calmly before feeding

Food is an important resource and also a good impulse control exercise.

Also because of the risk of injury, your dog should learn to wait calmly and at a distance until you release the food. Does your dog show food aggression? Then please feed him in a separate room or in the dog crate so that your child is not exposed to any danger. Don't leave his food on the floor if he hasn't finished.

6. Rules for playing

Who is the one who acts and who is the one who reacts? Does your dog constantly determine when and what is played? Do you always go for it? Keep that in mind and start making changes here as well.

7. Don`t allow hiding

It's not good if your dog hides under a table or the sofa.

Some dogs will then feel more secure and will start snapping if someone approaches when they are hiding. Allowing the dog to hide does not help the dog to get rid of his insecurity or fear.

In this case, put your dog on a house leash and take him to his safe place or crate.

8. No stalking allowed

You don't have to be controlled by your dog. You are very good at taking care of yourself. Also, this job is very tiring for your dog and he doesn't get the rest he needs. Since you are an independent person, you can also convey this to your dog.

Soon you will take on responsibility for another living being and your dog should not take on this responsibility.

When your dog starts paying the rent, do grocery shopping, and cleaning up, we can discuss that again.

9. Resting times

Please don't underestimate this point, especially when the baby is here and everything is new and exciting.

10. No jumping

It is important that your dog respects your personal space.

Soon you'll be walking around with your baby in your arms and it wouldn't be good if your dog jumped up on you. Otherwise use a house leash to help you.

Caution Danger: If you are pregnant and your belly is growing, your dog should under no circumstances jump on your belly!

Training before the baby comes

Now that we have established the foundation, we devote ourselves to the special topics of baby & dog. Practice with your dog while you are pregnant. This not only gives your dog security, but also you.

Exercises with a doll

You're holding a stuffed animal or baby doll and you're acting like it's your baby. In addition, you can play baby cries over loudspeakers.

How is your dog behaving?

Is he trying to jump up on you?

Does he let you out of his sight?

The aim of the exercise is for your dog to be able to relax even when you are with the doll. Practice different situations that will be part of everyday life in the future:

- Breastfeeding

- Walking around with the baby

- Changing diapers

You will not allow your dog to get excited around your baby. Excitement can quickly become dangerous. Aggression often arises from an increased level of excitement. But not only aggression can arise, but also barking, jumping or skipping actions. This can include chasing a tail, destroying something, or running around wildly. Send your dog out of your personal area and let him keep a distance of about 1m.

This is a good exercise to earn respect and show your dog that you are in charge.

Has your dog calmed down? Then you can walk up to him or call him over to you, and he can smell what you're holding on your arm from a safe distance.

Remember that you are rewarding calm & relaxed behavior. If your dog is in this state of mind, then he can do (almost) everything. He gets your trust and a lot of freedom.

Is the situation that you are walking around with something in your arms and your dog can not control himself? Then start with the dog resting place exercise. If your dog has associated the resting place with relaxation, you send him there and start practicing with the doll on your arm.

Important: Once you have sent your dog to his place, he must not leave there on his own. You won't release him until he's (at best) calm & relaxed.

Take up space

To claim a space for yourself, you need your body and your energy. Taking up space is normal among animals. Perhaps you yourself have already observed how a dog communicated with another dog from a distance. You can see this because when one dog has now decided to lay on the other dog's resting place and takes over.

If you have multiple dogs, or both a dog and a cat, at home, see how they use their body language, demeanor, and looks to communicate over a distance what's theirs and who wants what.

Since you claim your baby, you also control the space around your child. For this it is important that you know how to control your space.

Let's take the example that guests come to your house and the dog rushes towards them in the hallway.

Now how can you claim the guests and the door for yourself?

By standing in front of your visitor, with a firm footing. You can also put your hands on your hips or spread them out to the right and left. Sort of like pushing air away.

You now draw an invisible circle of about 1m around the door and around your visitor.

Your dog has to follow this invisible line. You only do that with your energy and your body.

For example, if you hold your dog by the collar or pull him away from the visitor, you are only controlling his body and not his mind. Your dog cannot understand what you want from him. In the worst case, you only reinforce his desire to get ahead or heat him up further.

Neither would any other dog. The dog leader in the pack would stand in front of or on top of what is his. His looks would be a definite warning to the other dogs. His body would be stiff, tail proud, and he would be planted with his paws firmly on the ground. He would clearly communicate with his body language and energy that this belongs to him.

If you have the opportunity, watch videos of herding dogs at work, how they communicate with the animals, who has to stay where. Pay attention to looks and body language.

Your calm and determined energy is again incredibly important here. If you are frustrated or angry, if you become loud, you have a weak energy for the dog. He can then not rely on you, follow you or listen to you.

Which people with which energy give you security, so that you would follow them?

Also try to develop composure. I know it's hard, but it's possible.

If you really mean it and communicate properly, you will be amazed at how quickly your dog accepts and respects it.

If it doesn't work, have someone film you and see how you come across in body language. Are you standing up straight? Are your shoulders back? Are you firmly on the ground? Would you follow yourself?

This is also an exercise that you can do in front of the mirror.

Your dog shows you exactly when your energy is convincing and when it isn't yet.

Please remember that most dogs are **not** natural leaders and do not intend to be. However, if they are not led, then they try to restore balance in the pack.

Somebody has to take care of security. Unfortunately, when this happens, a dog often acts out of frustration or fear. Most dogs do not know what is expected of them, they are overwhelmed with the role.

Take the lead, your dog will thank you!

claim toys or objects

Most likely, your child will have stuffed animals and toys. These belong to your child, not your dog. Before the baby arrives, start practicing with the things you don't want your dog to touch.

Claim them for yourself. Just like the previous exercise, except this time you don't claim the space, you claim an object.

Note: If you pull something away from your dog, then it will be even more exciting for him. He wants to chase or fight for it.

Please leave the objects, draw an invisible line around them (a taboo area), and your dog has to stay away.

Is this exercise is very difficult for your dog?

Here as well you can use the resting place exercise and send him there first.

You start playing with your child's things or just scattering them on the floor. Your dog can watch from its resting place and should learn to control itself.

The same applies e.g. with a playmat or other things that will be on the floor.

If your dog has learned before the baby arrives that these areas/objects are off-limits, you don't have to discuss it when the baby is there.

Another plus: Your dog will not associate these exercises with the baby.

If you have any doubts or begin to hesitate during the exercise, your dog will respond by continuing to challenge you to be clear.

To prevent frustration or obsession, it's important that you take the lead and set clear rules and boundaries for your dog. Many people worry that the dog might take offense at them.

Please do not forget: Your dog is an animal (predator). There are also rules and boundaries in the pack. This is natural for dogs and they also need this to be able to relax. As a leader you ensure their protection and well-being in return you get trust and respect.

Walking next to the stroller

Practice walking your dog on a loose leash next to the stroller in advance. If your dog finds the stroller scary, slowly get used to it. Here you can use food for motivation and for a positive connection.

Muzzle training

Since we don't know 100% how your dog will react to the baby and the new situations, muzzle training makes sense. Most owners (including me) find it difficult to put a muzzle on the dog. Make this a fun exercise with lots of muzzled treats. If you never need it, perfect! But if you do, then your dog has already had positive experiences with it. Think of the muzzle as a stress reliever: it relieves you of stress.

Baby- dog reunion

Giving birth for humans and dogs are very different. Let's first consider the birth of a human being.

It is often the case that the woman with labor and her partner come to the hospital.

There are then doctors, nurses, midwives, other parents-to-be,... Quite a lot of hustle and bustle. The baby is born under the supervision of specialist staff, is examined directly and the birth is celebrated. In the following days family & friends will come to congratulate, everyone wants to see the newborn.

How is it with dogs in contrast without human influence? A pregnant female dog withdraws from the pack and builds a den in the ground or finds a den. She gets the puppies there alone. The pack has to keep distance for the first few days. Gradually, the mother dog decides who from the pack is allowed to go to the puppies and support her in raising them.

The pack respects this and gives the mother dog and her puppies space and peace.

A big difference to us, right?

This means that the mother dog can decide when and who can see her puppies.

You can do that with your baby too!

I was lucky enough to be able to witness several dog births live.

At this point I would like to thank the breeders who let me observe their puppies/the pack.

What I saw were sovereign and strict mother dogs. They specifically prohibited the younger/wilder dogs in the pack from even approaching the puppies for the first few weeks.

Once the mother dog has the respect of the other dogs, she will gradually allow contact if the dogs are calm and polite.

I can assure you of one thing:

The assertive mother dog does not allow any excitement near her puppies.

So please do the same and stop excitement around your baby!

Why am I sharing this with you?

So that you know that it is very natural for you to keep your dog away from your child or set boundaries for them in the first place.

Many people feel guilty and do not want to exclude the dog. You can decide what you allow and when and what not. Trust your instincts. Your dog will respect if he respects you.

Coming home with the baby

Have you thought about where your dog will stay when the baby comes? Do you have family or friends watching? Or do you put him in a dog care for the time?

Be sure to practice this with your dog first. Let him sleep there several times so he can get used to it. Ask the supervisors to follow the new rules.

The big moment has come, you come home with your baby. Before the first contact, your dog should already have been physically active so that he is tired and calm. If you have the opportunity, greet your dog without the baby first.

Your dog and you will be excited to see each other again. This is not good energy for the first encounter with the baby.

After you have greeted each other extensively and your dog has calmed down, you can bring the baby.

As you have already practiced with the doll, you hold your child in your arms and your dog has to keep a polite distance.

If he is very calm and relaxed, you can let him approach you. Don't hold the baby right in front of him.

If he shows excitement, please stop it immediately. Think of the mom dog, no excitement near the puppies.

Be calm and determined yourself. No tension, nervousness or insecurity. Remember, your dog senses your mood.

If your dog is having a hard time, send him to his bed or crate. Give him a task and he can look at the baby, listen to it and above all smell it from a safe distance.

Don't worry, the dog's nose is so good that he can smell the baby even from a big distance.

If your dog shows signs of tension or stress, stop the situation and repeat it later when your dog has calmed down.

You can introduce your dog to the new smell before he even meets the baby. Take one of the baby's hats or blankets, claim it for yourself, and let your dog approach and sniff when it's quiet.

It is best to do this in a relaxed atmosphere. He is said to associate the smell directly with relaxation. Don't let him put the object in his mouth or play with it.

Here as well, polite behavior is desired.

In the best case, your dog now knows:

- Where his rest and safety zone is,

- Which areas & objects are taboo and

- That calm & relaxed behavior is desired.

He has learned to wait, to control himself and to pay attention to you. You are the leader and responsible for your little pack.

Your dog's job? To have a good time.

Example from training (true story)

A couple contacted me and we made an appointment to prepare the dog for the baby. We discussed all the important issues, but I never heard from the couple again.

A few months later I got a call from the couple: The baby was born. The man told me that he hadn't really kept to our agreements. He would have felt bad about setting boundaries for the dog and would rather have the dog decide freely. I thanked him for his honesty, just wondering why he had called in the first place.

The couple told me that it seemed to them that their dog had read my book. The dog is a very independent, older dog. He was very respectful, gave the space to mom and child, showed a lot of calmness and very polite behavior.

The couple would have liked to have the dog in the middle and close to the baby, but the dog didn't want to. They then asked me to make an appointment so I could look at the dog's behavior.

I visited the little family and what I saw was a relaxed dog that just wanted to be left alone. The couple tried too hard to get the dog in direct contact with the baby. They deliberately sought the closeness of the dog with the child, lured the dog to the child and absolutely wanted to establish contact between the two. Wanted the dog to lick the baby.

However, this can quickly end in a dangerous situation, which the parents obviously did not realize. Therefore, my request: Respect if your dog prefers to keep his distance. Do not lure him into the situations unnecessarily!

I could see this dog become even more suspicious after being lured. When we were sitting on the floor with the baby and he happened to be passing by, the couple tried so hard to get the dog to come to them until he ended up doing it for a short time just for his people. But the dog obviously didn't want to be there.

He preferred to keep his distance. Because the couple almost "forced" the baby on the dog, the dog started to already growl in one situation. It is important to realize that the dog did not make mistakes, but that people disregarded his communication.

So it was important for the good of both the child and the dog that the parents began to pay attention to and respect the dog's behavior.

What are your expectations?

Can you accept it if your dog behaves differently than you would like?

Can you read the signals?

Take care

It is important that you do not leave the dog and baby unattended. Even with the dearest dog, situations can arise that you could not have imagined before. The child can make uncontrolled movements and possibly hurt the dog.

The baby's grasping reflex may grab something and not let go. If the baby then grabs the dog's ear, for example, it is absolutely necessary for an adult to be able to open the hand again.

There were biting incidents where it later turned out that the child had put objects in the dog's body openings. At some point even the most patient dog can no longer do it. In older dogs, it can also happen that they suffer from age-related pain. We don't want the child to touch the wrong places and startle the dog. So caution is always required.

What to do if you can`t meet your dogs needs?

Do you feel like you can't meet your dog's needs? Your baby demands your full attention and your dog is neglected?

Your priorities have now shifted. You have a small, two-legged creature that is completely dependent on you. In addition, you also have your own needs that you should not forget.

If you get to this point, it would be good to have a plan B ready in advance.

<u>Dog daycare</u>

Is there a dog daycare near you? If your dog likes to be among its own kind, this is a way of knowing that it is being well looked after. Especially when things get too stressful for you. It is best for your dog to get to know the dog day care center before the baby moves in and get used to it. So your dog can have fun during the day and come home tired.

<u>Dog walking</u>

You don't have a dog daycare center nearby or your dog doesn't feel so comfortable there? How about a dog walker?

There your dog gets the exercise and fun it needs and can then relax at home with you.

Here as well it would be advisable to get used to it before the baby comes.

Neighbors

Do you have dog-loving neighbors where your dog is in good hands? Ask them for help when it gets too much for you.

Family and friends

The best solution, of course, is family and friends that your dog is already used to. Before the baby arrives, discuss what help you may need. Get your dog used to being with family or friends during the day or even overnight so it's normal for him.

You don't need to feel bad about temporarily housing your dog somewhere else. Make it a place where he's comfortable and having a good time. The baby and the new situation will also be stressful for your dog, so he deserves some vacation time. ☺

Influences from outside

It is often suggested in advertising or social media that dog and child means pure harmony. Unfortunately, many dog owners underestimate the fact that this often does not correspond to reality.

Supposedly cute photos and videos of babies & dogs are circulating on the Internet, which are described as cute. All I can say is that alarm bells are ringing for me.

For example, you see babies being placed on dogs even though the dog is clearly showing signs of stress.

Usually the dogs show beforehand that they do not feel comfortable with the situation. Since people often do not recognize these signs due to a lack of information, situations such as snapping or biting arise, which people often interpret as sudden, unpredictable and aggressive.

I can only recommend this: Learn to read and understand your dog!

Warnings of the dog can be e.g.:

- Avoid (e.g. turn your head away)

- Growl

- Keep still, become stiff

- Pull up lips, show teeth

It will most likely also happen to you that different people often want to give you advice about child and dog training without being asked. Don't let this unsettle you.

People don't know you, your baby, your dog, or your situation unless they are trained professionals, which in most cases is not the case. Every family is different in terms of their living situation, and even dogs cannot be lumped together because each dog is different.

Puppy & Baby

Admittedly, it's a nice idea when baby and puppy grow up together and become best friends.

However, it is often underestimated here that even a puppy means a lot of work. Raising a puppy and a baby at the same time can be extremely stressful. The puppy needs a lot of attention and your baby even more.

In the beginning, the puppy has to go out several times a day and night until it is housebroken. The world is explored with the mouth, possibly objects and furniture are nibbled on. The puppy wants to be trained and challenged, but also needs enough rest periods so that it doesn't overreact.

Of course, there are many positive examples where the families were able to deal very well with the double burden. Most of them were already experienced or have professional support. Or they're just lucky enough to have an easy-going dog who is forgiving of their owners' mistakes. Unfortunately, there are also many negative examples. It is imperative to protect the baby. Not to be neglected, by the way, is that the puppy is also protected from careless movements by the baby. Especially in the early puppy stages.

WORST CASE

This is a chapter I would like to skip. Unfortunately, it does happen, and that's why I want to be honest with you. Not every dog is suitable for living with a baby or child. In some cases, you might know before the baby is born if your dog will be ok with it or not.

If you notice that your dog shows these signs consistently, it indicates a lot of stress:

- Restlessness (constant running around)

- Panting

- They urinate and defecate in the apartment

- Vocalizations (whining, squeaking, barking)

- Whale eyes (whites can be seen in the corners of the eyes or above or below the eye on your dog)

- Feeling uncomfortable around the child (avoiding, threatening or even snapping)

- Rashes, loss of fur

- Frequent licking or scratching

Then it's time to think about finding a relaxing home for the dog. Maybe you have family or friends he already knows who would take him?

If not, then there are guaranteed to be lovely people who will take good care of your dog.

This isn't about someone failing. It's not the time for blame. We want you, your child and your dog to be well. A life of constant stress is not good for any living being.

In addition, you cannot expose your child to danger. It is defenseless, and bite wounds will mark it for life.

This is by no means an easy decision, but it is not the time to act selfishly.

Recommendations for the "worst case":

- Write a training diary and set a time window:

Set a window of time to work with your dog. Note the current status of his behavior. What are your goals? How much time can you take for the changes? Write a training diary so that you can assess the situation as best as possible after the time has elapsed.

- Who can train how much? Is that enough for your dog? Are your dog's needs met?

- Think early on: Are there friends/family who would take the dog?

- In the case of serious, existing problems, it is best to find a new home for the dog before the baby arrives.

- Seek timely support: You should have a trainer that you trust and who is available to you in an emergency.

Inside child & dog:

What a beautiful idea when child and dog grow up together. The child has in the dog a best friend, ally, comforter, confidant and playmate. Together they can discover the world, do silly things or just cuddle together. The child learns to take care of the dog and to take responsibility.

Unfortunately, this idea does not always correspond to reality. Even if we all want exactly that, there are dogs that - regardless of breed - are not suitable for this. Sadly, biting incidents involving children and often one's own dog are common.

Having a dog in the family means taking responsibility for a living being. The individual needs of the animal must be met for a relaxed coexistence. It is also important to mention here that the responsibility lies with the adults and not with the child!

Please note: Small children are not able to interpret the communication of the dogs and to react appropriately. They can't understand the dog's warnings.

Some dogs also have problems with toddlers' uncoordinated movements or vocalizations and don't know how to deal with them.

Child and dog can be a beautiful combination. However, there are also cases where the stress becomes too great and instead of harmony, stress prevails in everyday life.

The question arises whether there are child-friendly or family-friendly dog breeds.

Clearly: No! It always has to be looked at individually. There are breeds whose traits increase the likelihood that coexistence will work well, but there are no guarantees. Even a Labrador or Golden Retriever can dislike or even hurt children.

Child- Dog- Rules:

Unfortunately, accidents involving dogs with children are not uncommon, but many of them could have been prevented.

Learn to read your dog, pay attention to body language and teach the children to treat animals with respect. Here you will find important rules for the coexistence of children and dogs.

You should start early on to convey it to your children as well as to the guest children. Cut out the following rules and hang them on the fridge, for example.

1. Always wait for the adult to engage with the dog!

2. Ask if it's ok and if the dog wants it too.

3. Don't kiss the dog.

4. Don't hug the dog.

5. Approach from the side and let the dog sniff first. If the dog doesn't want that, leave him alone.

6. Never run after a dog.

7. Do not touch the dog directly on the head, it is better to pet it under the chin or on the back.

8. If a dog is nearby, don't run wild, yell, or suddenly throw up your arms.

9. The dog's resting place is absolutely taboo!

10. Don't take food away from the dog and don't reach into the food bowl!

Conclusion

If rules are set in good time and the dog's needs are met, nothing should stand in the way of a relaxed family life.

The resting place, the dog crate and the children's gate are particularly important for the crawling age. Your dog should always be able to relax there.

Always pay attention to your dog's body language, especially towards the child. Can you see tension or is everything relaxed?

Please trust your gut feeling and get help if you are unsure.

Please never leave your dog and child alone!

Finally, I wish you a lot of joy with baby & dog!

Attachment

Training table

Enter the date, time, exercise, number of repetitions, duration of the session and your notes.

What went well and what not so well? This gives you a good overview of your training and progress.

Set yourself small goals during training that you can achieve step by step.

Date	Time	Exercise	Number of repetitions	Duration	Notes +/-	

Date	Time	Exercise	Number of repetitions	Duration	Notes +/-

Date	Time	Exercise	Number of repetitions	Duration	Notes +/-

Date	Time	Exercise	Number of repetitions	Duration	Notes +/-

Date	Time	Exercise	Number of repetitions	Duration	Notes +/-

Date	Time	Exercise	Number of repetitions	Duration	Notes +/-	

Date	Time	Exercise	Number of repetitions	Duration	Notes +/-	

Date	Time	Exercise	Number of repetitions	Duration	Notes +/-

Date	Time	Exercise	Number of repetitions	Duration	Notes +/-	

Date	Time	Exercise	Number of repetitions	Duration	Notes +/-

Date	Time	Exercise	Number of repetitions	Duration	Notes +/-

Date	Time	Exercise	Number of repetitions	Duration	Notes +/-

Notizen

....
....
....
....
....
....
....
....
....
....
....
....
....
....
....
....
....
....
....
....
....
....
....
....
....
....
....

....
....
....
....
....
....
....
....
....
....
....
....
....
....
....
....
....
....
....
....
....
....
....
....
....
....
....
....
....
....
....
....

Thank you for your support:

Bianca,

Katharina,

Nina, Bernardo, Noah mit Nelly,

Pazit

Sabine und

Tobi, Juna mit Mina.